The Berenstain Bears'
SCIENCE FAIR

The bears are going to have a science fair.
Small Bear and Sister want to make something
for the fair. This is a good time for Papa
to give them some science lessons.

Published in the United States by Random House, Inc., New York, and simultaneously in Canada
by Random House of Canada Limited, Toronto.
Library of Congress Cataloging in Publication Data
Berenstain, Stanley. The Berenstain Bears' science fair. SUMMARY: Papa Bear teaches
Small Bear and Sister about machines, matter, and energy, and helps them prepare projects for science fair.
  1. Science—Juvenile literature.   2. Science—Exhibitions—Juvenile literature.   [1. Science] I. Berenstain,
Janice,   joint author.   II. Title.   Q163.B498   500   76-8121   ISBN 0-394-93294-3 lb. bdg.   ISBN 0-394-83294-9
Manufactured in the United States of America   2 3 4 5 6 7 8 9 0

To make a good project
for the Bears' Science Fair,
you must learn about science.
Follow me, Sister! Come along, Small Bear!

As an old science student
I know just where to start . . .

It's lucky for us, Dad,
that you are so smart!

DANGER
MACHINES
AT
WORK

6

To teach science well,
to make science fun,
I start with *machines*! . . .
Put on a safety hat, Son!

DANGER
MACHINES
AT
WORK

And here's your first lesson—
Be very careful near a machine!

Right, Papa Bear.
We see what you mean.

7

ACTUAL FACTS ABOUT MACHINES

WHAT IS A MACHINE?

A machine is a thing we use to help us do work.

There are machines that help us do tough, rough jobs—

There are machines that help us do fine, exact work—

My sewing machine makes perfect stitches!

There are almost as many kinds of machines as there are kinds of work.

But big or small or in between, if it helps you do work, then it's a **MACHINE!**

FINE SEWING

THREE SIMPLE MACHINES

Now the three most important
machines, I feel,
are the simple **lever**,
the **wedge** and the **wheel**.

1. THE LEVER

Press down here

to lift up here.

WHEN A POLE OR
BAR IS USED TO LIFT
OR PRY, IT BECOMES
A LEVER.

Ahem! . . .

11

I like to make posters.
Here's how I do it—

See this big piece of cardboard
with pictures stuck to it?

LEVERS

A
SCIENCE FAIR POSTER
by Sister Bear

WE USE LEVERS
IN MANY WAYS—

TO OPEN CANS...

JARS...

AND BOTTLES...

jack

TO LIFT CARS...

TO STOP CARS...

brake

TO PUMP WATER.

The lever lifts up here.

You push down here.

Water comes out here.

SOMETIMES WE USE
TWO LEVERS TOGETHER—

TO CRACK NUTS...

TO CLIP TOENAILS...

TO SQUEEZE
ORANGES.

MANY TOOLS ARE LEVERS—

pliers

wrench

hammer

We use levers every day.
They make hard jobs easier
and they let us do things we're
not strong enough to do ourselves.

13

2. THE WEDGE

Push down here...

to split or spread log here.

THE WEDGE IS USED TO SPLIT THINGS OR TO SPREAD THINGS APART.

The **wedge** has many uses.
Splitting logs is one.
Our friendly neighbor, Farmer Ben,
will show us how it's done.

WOK!

Thank you, Ben.
As I said before,
that's one of its uses.
It has many more!

OTHER WAYS WE USE THE WEDGE

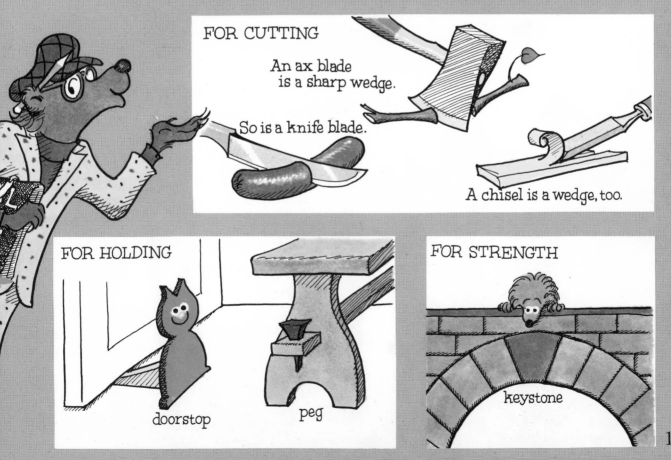

FOR CUTTING

An ax blade
is a sharp wedge.

So is a knife blade.

A chisel is a wedge, too.

FOR HOLDING

doorstop

peg

FOR STRENGTH

keystone

15

Now here is a tool
that's both lever _and_ wedge!

scythe

The handle's a lever.
The blade is a wedge.

It cuts weeds fast
with a stroke that's neat.

That certainly was
both fast and neat.
But you didn't cut weeds.
You cut Farmer Ben's wheat!

A simple machine
we use a good deal
is our greatest invention.
It's called THE WHEEL!

3. THE WHEEL

Turn this way...   to go this way.

axle

A WHEEL IS ROUND.
IT TURNS AROUND
A ROD CALLED AN AXLE
THAT RUNS THROUGH
THE CENTER.

Here we have wheels of every kind.
Let's see how many we can find.

wagon wheel

auto wheel

truck wheel

train wheel

water wheel

paddle wheel

ship's wheel

plane wheel

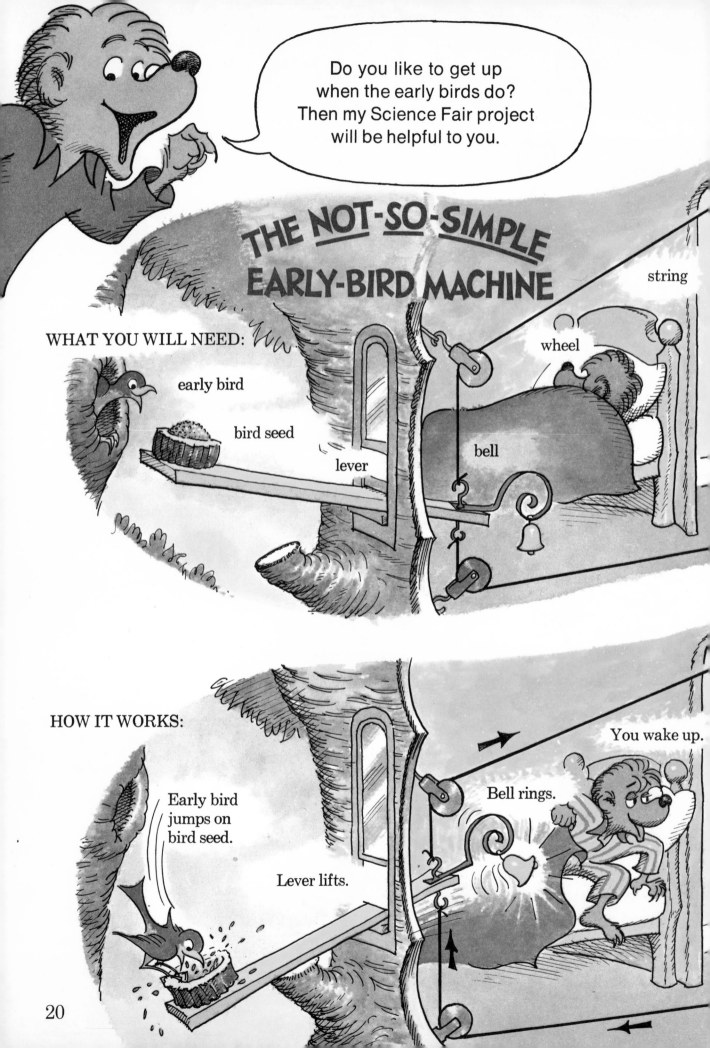

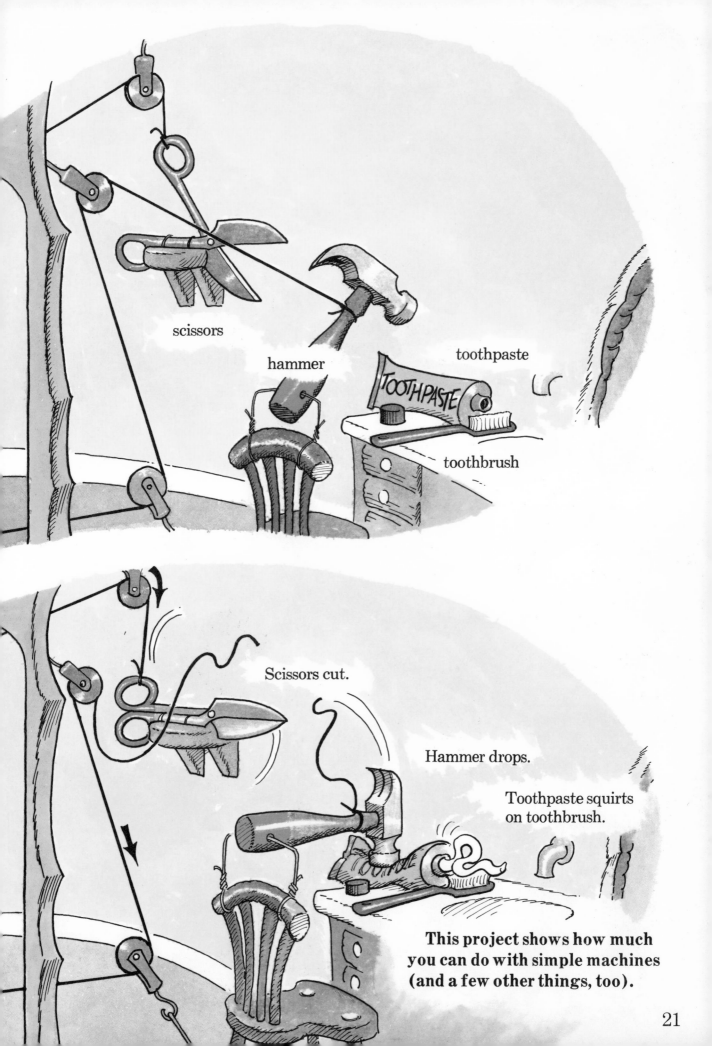

scissors

hammer

toothpaste

TOOTHPASTE

toothbrush

Scissors cut.

Hammer drops.

Toothpaste squirts
on toothbrush.

**This project shows how much
you can do with simple machines
(and a few other things, too).**

21

But, Papa! . . .
Look over there!
They're getting ready
for the Science Fair.

We have lots of time.
Just stop the chatter.
I still have to teach you
some facts about **matter**.

23

THE THREE KINDS OF MATTER

I still remember from my science class that matter can be **solid** or **liquid** or **gas**.

1. SOLID

A PIECE OF MATTER THAT KEEPS ITS SHAPE IS CALLED A SOLID.

There are many solids.
They're all around—
those rocks, that sign,
this road, the ground . . .

Now what other solids
do we see?

SHARP
CURVE

That tree! Papa Bear.
Look out for that tree!

Wow! That was some solid,
that giant oak tree.

Yes. That was a solid.
I do agree.

While Mom and Dad
are making repairs,
let's name some solids
with the two little bears.

ACTUAL
FACTUAL
BEAR

HOW MANY SOLIDS CAN WE NAME?

Hmm...
Let's see.

wood

metal

glass

plastic

Rubber's a solid that is elastic!

29

We're partly solids.

claw

tooth

muscle

bone

So is the earth.

sand

soil

clay

stone

We wear some solids.

straw

shell

cotton

feather

gold

wool

nylon

leather

Some solids we <u>eat</u>.

meat

sugar

chocolate

cheese

hard-boiled egg

pudding

peas

SOLIDS ARE MOST OF THE THINGS WE HAVE KNOWN.

SOLIDS ALL HAVE A SHAPE OF THEIR OWN.

2. LIQUID

LIQUID IS MATTER THAT HAS NO SHAPE OF ITS OWN. IT FLOWS AND POURS.

Are we ready for liquids?
Ah! I see that you are.
Without liquids to drink,
we wouldn't get far.

The most useful liquid—
Are you listening, Daughter?
The most useful liquid . . .

...is the one we call WATER!

WATER
AND HOW WE USE IT

FOR DRINKING
We use water from rivers and streams and underground wells.

WATER WORKS

ACTUAL FACTUAL BEAR

FOR TRANSPORTATION
By using boats, we can travel wherever there is enough water.

FOR RAISING FOOD
Plants won't grow without it.

FOR WASHING
We can't keep clean
without water.

FOR FIGHTING FIRES
Water can put out
most fires.

FIRE BOAT

FOR KEEPING COOL
A-a-a-ah!

MILL

FOR POWER
Water flowing downhill turns
waterwheels. This wheel
is turning a grindstone
that grinds wheat into flour.

35

The most useful liquid
is water, it's true.
But other liquids
are useful, too.

OTHER USEFUL LIQUIDS

GASOLINE makes motors go.

OIL makes them run smoothly.

DYE colors cloth.

ALCOHOL kills germs.

Some liquids are useful because
they harden into solids.

glue

nail polish

concrete

3. GAS

GAS IS MATTER
THAT HAS NO SHAPE
AT ALL. IT CAN BE
COLLECTED IN A CLOSED
CONTAINER, OR IT
CAN SPREAD OUT IN
THE AIR.

A gas balloon!
Lucky for us
we happened to pass!
This is our chance
to learn about gas.

But, Papa, that sign
makes it very clear.
There may be a chance
of some danger here!

Not for a gas
expert like me!
To understand gases,
use this as a key:

Solids and liquids take up
a limited space.
But gases spread out
all over the place.

There's helium gas
in this small tank.
Hmmm ... I wonder
what happens
when you turn the crank.

The balloon goes up!
That's what happens, Pop.
And I do not think
it is going to stop!

Papa!
What makes it fly?
What makes the balloon
go up so high?

A very good question,
Sister Bear!
Helium gas
is lighter than air!

39

41

The THREE KINDS OF MATTER are what you will see when you do this science experiment with me.

1 Start with ice.

Ice is a SOLID. ————

It has weight. It takes up space. And ice has a shape of its own.

2 Take ice from the freezer.

Let it melt.

3 It will all change to water.

Water is a LIQUID.

It still has weight.
It still takes up space...

but it no longer has
a shape of its own.
It flows and pours.

42

4 Next, heat the water.

5 Let it boil.

6 It will all change to steam.

Steam is a GAS.

It still has weight.
It still takes up space.
But now it has no shape at all!

Now you know that matter
can change its form
when the temperature gets
a little too warm.

Note: Not all solids are as easy to change
as ice, but all solids—even rock—will
change if they get hot enough.

43

THE THREE KINDS
OF MATTER:
SOLID, LIQUID
& GAS.

Thank you, Papa.
Those lessons were fun.
We really appreciate
all you have done.

And thanks to your
lessons, Papa Bear,
we all have good projects
for the fair!

NOT-SO-SIMPLE
EARLY-BIRD MACHINE

LEVE

That's right, Small Bear,
the three of you do—
but I plan to make
a project, too.
So, hold everything now,
and wait for me!

You still have to learn
about **energy**!

BEFORE ENERGY LESSON NUMBER ONE, A BRIEF COMMERCIAL FOR THE SUN:

Most of our energy comes to us from the sun. It comes to us in the form of light.

Sunlight warms the earth.

The sun's light also keeps our planet green.

Heat and light make our planet a good place to live.

WITHOUT THE SUN, EARTH WOULDN'T BE MUCH OF A PLACE— JUST A BIG, COLD ROCK FLOATING IN SPACE.

END OF COMMERCIAL!

ACTUAL FACTS ABOUT ENERGY

WHAT IS ENERGY?

Energy is what it takes
to get things done!

Any kind of work or play
takes **ENERGY**, my son.

Energy is the "go" of things.
Without energy to make things happen,
there would be no movement or change.

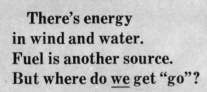

SOURCES OF ENERGY

There's energy
in wind and water.
Fuel is another source.
But where do <u>we</u> get "go"?

We get it from food,
of course.

THE BURGER BEAR

1. ENERGY FROM FOOD

OUR BODIES TURN
THE FOOD WE EAT
INTO THE ENERGY
WE NEED TO WORK
AND PLAY.

Four burgers, please.
And if it isn't
too much trouble,
make mine a Papa Bear
super-double!

THE BURGE

48

HOW OUR BODIES TURN FOOD INTO ENERGY

Teeth chew food into small pieces. It travels to the stomach, where it is dissolved by stomach juices.

Dissolved food passes into the bloodstream.

It is now ready to be used as energy.

If we eat more than we need it is stored in the body as fat!

So I'm not overweight, you see, I just have too much energy!

2. ENERGY FROM FUEL

THERE IS ENERGY IN MATTER. FUEL IS MATTER THAT IS BURNED TO GET ENERGY.

Wow!
There's sure a lot of "go"
going on down there!

And almost all of it
comes from fuel, Small Bear.

The most important fuels are oil, coal and natural gas. They were made in the earth millions of years ago.

It takes a long time for the earth to make fuels—a lot longer than it takes us to use them up. So be careful not to waste them.

51

ENERGY FROM
3. WIND and WATER

MOVING AIR AND
MOVING WATER
CAN GIVE US
USEFUL ENERGY.

Wind is moving air.
It can be very strong.
It can push a sailboat
right along.

That is very
interesting, Pop.
But it's pushing this sailboat
toward quite a drop!

Well, don't just stand
around and look!
Help me with
this grappling hook.

HOW WE USE WATER
TO MAKE ELECTRICITY

A wall is built
across a swift stream.

It is called a dam.

Water builds up
behind the dam.
Some of it is
allowed to spill over.

This falling water turns
waterwheels that run special
machines called generators.
These change the energy
of the falling water into
electrical energy.

This electrical energy
comes to us over wires.

To make a special
high-flying jet,
here is what
you have to get:
a balloon—
any color, size or shape—
a piece of paper
and some tape.

1 Make a paper airplane.

FOLD   FOLD

FOLD

2 Make a loop of tape
(sticky side out).

Stick it to the airplane.

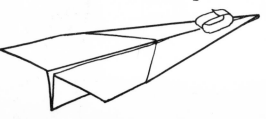

3 Take a deep Papa Bear breath
and blow up the balloon.

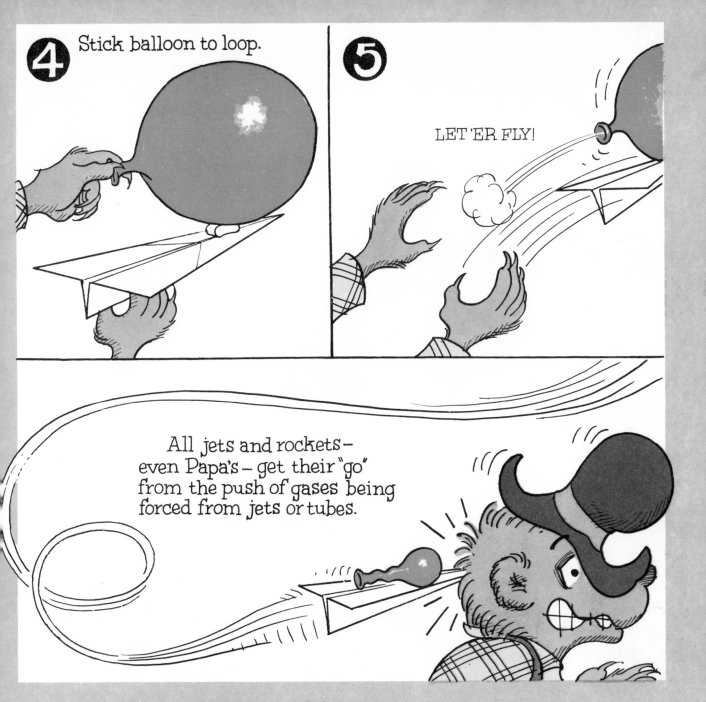

4 Stick balloon to loop.

5 LET 'ER FLY!

All jets and rockets—
even Papa's—get their "go"
from the push of gases being
forced from jets or tubes.

**It's fun to experiment with jet power.
Here are some more high-fliers.**

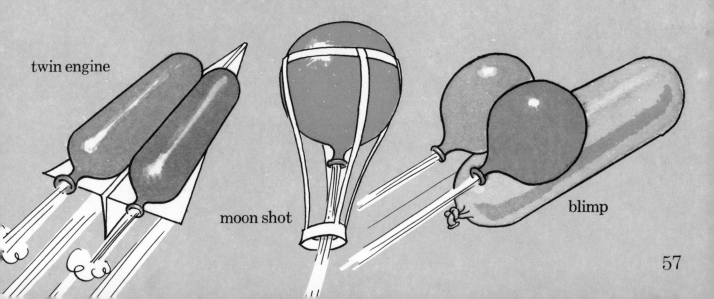

twin engine

moon shot

blimp

Now we all
have projects
to show.
Come, Papa Bear.
Let us go!

We really love
your lessons, Pop.
But isn't it time
for them to—

STOP!

No more time for talk,
Small Bear!
They're about to start . . .

At last! ... And as soon as the Bear Family sets up its projects, The Bears' Science Fair will be officially open.